D0965654

THIS JOURNAL BELONGS TO:

_____

DATE:

_____

The challenge of life is to take
a single strand of a dream
and from it weave a beautiful reality.

I still find each day too short for all the thoughts
I want to think, all the walks I want to take....
The longer I live, the more my mind dwells upon
the beauty and the wonder of the world.
JOHN BURROUGHS

As the years pass, I am coming more and more to understand
that it is the common, everyday blessings of our common
everyday lives for which we should be particularly grateful.
LAURA INGALLS WILDER

Live your life while you have it.
Life is a splendid gift—
there is nothing small about it.
FLORENCE NIGHTINGALE

Encourage one another daily, as long as it is called "Today."
THE BIBLE

Gratitude bestows reverence, allowing us
to encounter everyday epiphanies, those
transcendent moments of awe that change
forever how we experience life and the world.

JOHN MILTON

Some people see things as they are and ask, "Why?"
I dream things as they never were and ask, "Why not?"
GEORGE BERNARD SHAW

> Our Creator would never have made such lovely days,
> and have given us the deep hearts to enjoy them,
> above and beyond all thought,
> unless we were meant to be immortal.
> NATHANIEL HAWTHORNE

Today is unique! It has never occurred before, and it will never be repeated. At midnight it will end, quietly, suddenly, totally. Forever. But the hours between now and then are opportunities with eternal possibilities.
CHARLES R. SWINDOLL

Lord...teach me to live this moment only,
looking neither to the past with regret,
nor the future with apprehension.
Let love be my aim and my life a prayer.
ROSEANN ALEXANDER-ISHAM

We are weaving the future on the loom of today.
GRACE STRICKER DAWSON

Every day we live is a priceless gift of God,
loaded with possibilities to learn something new,
to gain fresh insights.
DALE EVANS ROGERS

I have learned from experience that the greater part
of our happiness or misery depends on our dispositions
and not on our circumstances.
MARTHA WASHINGTON

> You will find as you look back upon your life,
> that the moments when you have really lived
> are the moments when you have
> done things in the spirit of love.
>
> HENRY DRUMMOND

Nature decrees that we do not exceed the speed of light.
All other impossibilities are optional.
ROBERT BRAULT

Everything in life is most fundamentally a gift.
And you receive it best, and you live it best,
by holding it with very open hands.

LEO O'DONOVAN

God not only loves you very much but also
has put his hand on you for something special.
THE BIBLE

Isn't it splendid to think of all the things there are to find out about? It just makes me feel glad to be alive—it's such an interesting world. It wouldn't be half so interesting if we knew all about everything.

LUCY MAUD MONTGOMERY

What we feel, think, and do this moment influences both
our present and the future in ways we may never know. Begin.
Start right where you are. Consider your possibilities and find
inspiration…to add more meaning and zest to your life.
ALEXANDRA STODDARD

Dear Lord, grant me the grace of wonder. Surprise me, amaze me, awe me in every crevice of Your universe.... Each day enrapture me with Your marvelous things without number. I do not ask to see the reason for it all; I ask only to share the wonder of it all.

ABRAHAM JOSHUA HESCHEL

Slow down and enjoy life. It's not only the scenery
you miss by going too fast—you also miss the sense
of where you are going and why.
EDDIE CANTOR

Whether sixty or sixteen, there is in every human being's heart the love of wonder, the sweet amazement at the stars and starlike things, the undaunted challenge of events, the unfailing childlike appetite for what-next, and the joy of the game of living.

SAMUEL ULLMAN

A strong positive mental attitude will create more miracles
than any wonder drug.
PATRICIA NEAL

God puts each fresh morning,
each new chance of life,
into our hands as a gift to see
what we will do with it.

ANONYMOUS

When we take time to notice the simple things in life,
we never lack for encouragement. We discover
we are surrounded by a limitless hope
that's just wearing everyday clothes.
WENDY MOORE

Some days, it is enough encouragement
just to watch the clouds break up and disappear,
leaving behind a blue patch of sky and bright
sunshine that is so warm upon my face.
It's a glimpse of divinity; a kiss from heaven.

ANONYMOUS

"For I know the plans I have for you," declares the Lord,
"plans to prosper you and not to harm you,
plans to give you hope and a future."
THE BIBLE

Most folks are about as happy
as they make up their minds to be.
ABRAHAM LINCOLN

Joy cannot be pursued. It comes from within.
It is a state of being. It does not depend on circumstances,
but triumphs over circumstances. It produces a gentleness
of spirit and a magnetic personality.
BILLY GRAHAM

In ordinary life we hardly realize that we receive a great deal more than we give, and that it is only with gratitude that life becomes rich.

DIETRICH BONHOEFFER

God gave you a gift of 86,400 seconds today.
WILLIAM ARTHUR WARD

Life is not a journey to the grave with the intention of arriving safely in one pretty and well-preserved piece, but to skid across the line broadside, thoroughly used up, worn out, leaking oil, shouting Geronimo!

BILL MCKENNA

See each morning a world made anew, as if it were
the morning of the very first day. Treasure and use it,
as if it were the final hour of the very last day.
FAY HARTZELL ARNOLD

All we have to decide is what to do
with the time that is given to us.
J. R. R. TOLKIEN

Look deep within yourself and recognize
what brings life and grace into your heart.
It is this that can be shared with those around you.
CHRISTOPHER DE VINCK

What a wildly wonderful world,
God! You made it all.
THE BIBLE

A joyful spirit is like a sunny day; it sheds
a brightness over everything; it sweetens
our circumstances and soothes our souls.
ANONYMOUS

In the process of creation and relationship,
what seems mundane and trivial may show itself
to be holy, precious, part of a pattern.
LUCI SHAW

My advice is, never do tomorrow what you can do today.
Procrastination is the thief of time.
CHARLES DICKENS

I think miracles exist in part as gifts
and in part as clues that there is something
beyond the flat world we see.
PEGGY NOONAN

To be glad of life, because it gives you the chance to love
and to work and to play and to look up at the stars;
to be satisfied with your possessions, but not content...
until you have made the best of them...
these are little guideposts on the footpath to peace.
HENRY VAN DYKE

All that we have and are is one of the unique
and never-to-be repeated ways God has chosen
to express Himself in space and time.

BRENNAN MANNING

The joy that you give to others is the joy
that comes back to you.
JOHN GREENLEAF WHITTIER

Begin today! No matter how feeble the light,
let it shine as best it may. The world may need
just that quality of light which you have.

HENRY C. BLINN

Each day is a treasure box of gifts from God,
just waiting to be opened.
Open your gifts with excitement.
JOAN CLAYTON

Life begins each morning....
Each morning is the open door to a new world—
new vistas, new aims, new tryings.
LEIGH MITCHELL HODGES

A kind heart is a fountain of gladness,
making everything in its vicinity freshen into smiles.
WASHINGTON IRVING

Each dawn holds a new hope for a new plan,
making the start of each day the start of a new life.
GINA BLAIR

With God all things are possible.
THE BIBLE

The best and most beautiful things in the world
cannot be seen or even touched.
They must be felt with the heart.
HELEN KELLER

All enjoyment spontaneously overflows into praise.
C. S. LEWIS

There are only two ways to live your life.
One is as though nothing is a miracle.
The other is as though everything is a miracle.

RICHARD CRASHAW

This bright, new day, complete with twenty-four hours
of opportunities, choices, and attitudes, comes with a perfectly
matched set of 1,440 minutes. This unique gift, this one day,
cannot be exchanged, replaced, or refunded. Handle with care.
ANONYMOUS

HOPE is the ability to hear the music of the future....
FAITH is having the courage to dance to it today.

PETER KUZMIC

Live for today but hold your hands open to tomorrow.
Anticipate the future and its changes with joy.
Barbara Johnson

Now these three remain: faith, hope, and love.
But the greatest of these is love. Follow the way of love.

THE BIBLE

May you live all the days of your life.
JONATHAN SWIFT

> The patterns of our days are always rearranging…
> and each design for living is unique,
> graced with its own special beauty.
>
> ANONYMOUS

May our lives be illumined
by the steady radiance
renewed daily,
of a wonder,
the source of which
is beyond reason.
DAG HAMMARSKJÖLD

Just as there comes a warm sunbeam into
every cottage window, so comes a love—
born of God's care for every separate need.
NATHANIEL HAWTHORNE

Live today fully, expressing gratitude for all you have been,
all you are right now, and all you are becoming.
MELODY BEATTIE

Love wholeheartedly, be surprised,
give thanks and praise—then you will
discover the fullness of your life.
DAVID STEINDL-RAST

Celebrate God all day, every day. I mean, *revel* in him!
THE BIBLE

> Normal day, let me be aware of the treasure you are.
> Let me learn from you, love you, bless you before
> you depart. Let me not pass you by in quest
> of some rare and perfect tomorrow.
> MARY JEAN IRION

Wherever you go, no matter what the weather,
always bring your own sunshine.
ANTHONY D'ANGELO

All the things in this world are gifts
and signs of God's love to us.
The whole world is a love letter from God.

PETER KREEFT

I think what we're longing for is not "the good life"
as it's been advertised to us...but life in its fullness,
its richness, its abundance. Living more reflectively
helps us enter into that fullness.
KEN GIRE

> Wholehearted, ready laughter heals, encourages, relaxes anyone within hearing distance. The laughter that springs from love makes wide the space around it—gives room for the loved one to enter in.
>
> EUGENIA PRICE

Gratitude can transform common days into thanksgivings,
turn routine jobs into joy, and change ordinary
opportunities into blessings.
WILLIAM ARTHUR WARD

We need to recapture the power of imagination;
we shall find that life can be full of wonder,
mystery, beauty, and joy.

SIR HAROLD SPENCER JONES

The uncertainties of the present always give way
to the enchanted possibilities of the future.
GELSEY KIRKLAND

Some blessings—like rainbows after rain
or a friend's listening ear—are extraordinary gifts
waiting to be discovered in an ordinary day.
ANONYMOUS

Tuck [this] thought into your heart today.
Treasure it. Your Father God cares about
your daily everythings that concern you.
KAY ARTHUR

> Think excitement, talk excitement, act out excitement, and you are bound to become an excited person. Life will take on a new zest, deeper interest, and greater meaning.
> NORMAN VINCENT PEALE

A positive attitude may not solve all your problems,
but it will annoy enough people to make it worth the effort.
HERM ALBRIGHT

Always new. Always exciting. Always full of promise.
The mornings of our lives, each a personal daily miracle!
GLORIA GAITHER

The wonder of living is held within the beauty
of silence, the glory of sunlight…the sweetness
of fresh spring air, the quiet strength of earth,
and the love that lies at the very root of all things.

ANONYMOUS

The innocent brightness of a new born day is lovely yet.
WILLIAM WORDSWORTH

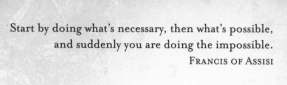

Start by doing what's necessary, then what's possible,
and suddenly you are doing the impossible.
FRANCIS OF ASSISI

Ellie Claire® Gift & Paper Expressions
Franklin, TN 37067
EllieClaire.com
Ellie Claire is a registered trademark of Worthy Media, Inc.

Today Is Going to Be Ridiculously Amazing! Journal
© 2016 by Ellie Claire
Published by Ellie Claire, an imprint of Worthy Publishing Group,
a division of Worthy Media, Inc.

ISBN 978-1-63326-101-3

Stock or custom editions of Ellie Claire titles may be purchased in bulk for educational,
business, ministry, fundraising, or sales promotional use. For information, please email
info@EllieClaire.com

Cover and interior design by Gearbox | studiogearbox.com

Printed in China

6 7 8 9 10 11 12 13 14 – 23 22 21 20 19 18